Abused But Not Shaken

A Christian Response to Domestic Violence And Abuse

By Dr. Patricia Diann Heathman

Revised

Abused But Not Shaken
A Christian Response to Domestic Violence And Abuse

Revised

By Dr. Patricia Diann Heathman

Copyright © 2007 by Patricia D. Heathman, D.D.
All Rights Reserved

All rights reserved under international copyright laws.
No portion of this book may be reproduced without the express written consent of the publisher.

Unless otherwise indicated, all scripture quotations
are taken from the Holy Bible Amplified Version
Copyright © 1973, 1978, 1984
The International Bible Society.
Used by permission of Zondervan Bible Publishers
All Rights Reserved.

Voice of The Spirit
Pontiac, Michigan

Dedicated To...
My mother, Dorothy Johnson, who raised her children in spite of her circumstances.

To my loving grandmother, Irene Briggs, who introduced me to Christ

And to my daughters, Selina and NA'Arah.

Foreword
By Dr. Gregory Heathman

While ministering in the Sunday evening worship service at our local church, Pat both shocked and blessed the Body when she departed from her prepared message and began to share the very personal story of her life growing up, as a child, in a violent home.

Her honesty and candor both surprised and blessed the people of God as she, with tears streaming down her cheeks, told of watching helplessly as her stepfather brutally beat and abused her mother.

Pat told of how growing up in an atmosphere where she witnessed alcohol abuse and physical violence, on a regular basis, made her a frightened, nervous child. In fact, she was so traumatized by the time she reached twelve years of age, that doctors wanted to put her on medication to calm and control her nerves and anxiety.

Pat went on to tell how her faith in God sustained her through the most trying of times. She told the gathering of Believers how, through the power of the Holy Spirit, she overcame her circumstances to become the woman of God that she is today.

When Pat finished speaking, that evening, those who had been smiling through pain filled the altar seeking healing and deliverance.

This book comes out of Pat's desire to take the message of healing and hope to hurting people the world over. The story of how God pulled triumph out of tragedy in one woman's life will inform, lift and inspire.

Table of Contents

Chapter 1
What is Domestic Violence?   7

Chapter 2
The Saga Continues   15

Chapter 3
Childhood Tears and Fears   21

Chapter 4
Emotional Hang-Ups   29

Chapter 5
Stop Blaming Yourself   43

Chapter 6
Receive Your Healing   47

Chapter 7
Walk In Victory   59

Chapter 8
Life Is Not Over   67

1

What Is Domestic Abuse?

According to the American Heritage *Dictionary, abuse is, "To use wrongly or improperly; misuse. To hurt or injure by maltreatment; ill use; to assail with contemptuous, coarse, or insulting words, revile. Physical maltreatment. Insulting or coarse language."*

Abuse, in one form or another, takes place everywhere. In the workplace, in our schools, in nursing homes, prisons and even in churches. It is called domestic abuse when it occurs between persons who live in the same household. This includes married couples and unmarried persons who share a home. It also includes the abuse of children and the abuse of parents or elders. While men usually direct domestic abuse at women, the reverse is not unheard of.

Domestic abuse is almost always about gaining and maintaining control and power over another person. An abuser may use a variety of tactics in an effort to dominate and hold sway over the life of the victim.

Emotional Abuse

Emotional or verbal abuse is the use of insults, name-calling, humiliation and etc. to harass and intimidate another person. The aim of emotional/verbal abuse is to gain and maintain control over the victim by destroying his or her confidence and self-esteem.

Many survivors report having undergone mind games, public embarrassment and manipulations that have left enduring emotional scars. As we know, emotional scars can remain long after physical scars have been healed.

Isolation

Keeping a victim isolated from family and friends is a common practice among abusers. This leads to the victim feeling helpless and totally dependent upon the abuser. It also helps perpetuate the abuse by keeping it hidden from people who may be inclined to intervene.

When asked, "Why do you stay?" victims often tell of being kept isolated to the point of thinking that no one else cared so where would they go? What would they do?

Threats and Intimidation

"If you open your mouth to anyone, I'll kill you!" or, "If you want to see the little rug rats of yours again, you'd better do what I say!" are words that are often used by abusers to strike fear into the hearts of their victims. Some abusers may even use threats of suicide to keep the victim from trying to escape an abusive relationship.

Physical Violence

Studies show that in these relationships, the abuse tends to escalate in spite of the victims attempts to comply with the wishes of the abuser.

Verbal abuse, threats and intimidation are often indicators of potential physical abuse. Studies demonstrate that once the violence begins it will not end until the abuser gets help, or the victim escapes. Regrettably, in many cases, the abuse only ends with the tragic death of the victim, the abuser or both.

Economic Depravity

Economic depravity and "male privilege" are also common abuse tactics. Economic depravity involves restricting the victim's access to money as a means of maintaining control.

An abusive spouse, for example, may forbid the victim from holding a job. He may even harass the victim on the job. Eventually, the situation becomes so uncomfortable and frightening that the company has no choice but to let the victim go.

The abuser wants the victim to be totally dependent upon him for everything. He can then use this dependence to control the victim's life.

Male Privilege

Male privilege involves a man exercising control over a woman by fostering a "me king, you servant" relationship. A relationship in which the victim is treated more like a slave than a partner. This, perhaps, is the most common abuse tactic used by religious men.

Many religious men, including some Christian men, twist the doctrine of male responsibility and headship until it no longer resembles anything found in the Bible. Then they use their twisted interpretation to heap abuse upon their unwitting wives and children.

Ephesians 5:22-24 is the passage most often "misused" in an effort to prop up the unbiblical doctrine of male privilege.

> *Wives, submit yourselves unto your own husbands, as unto the Lord. For the husband is the head of the wife, even as Christ is the head of the church: and he is the savior of the body. Therefore as the church is subject unto Christ, so let the wives be to their own husbands in every thing. (KJV)*

The term "submit" in this verse means the wife is to cooperate with her husband as he attempts to walk in his divinely assigned role of provider and protector. It does not suggest the husband has a right to make a slave of the wife.

Another thing to note about the verse is that while it does tell the wife to submit, it does not tell the husband to force or beat her into submission. True submission is voluntary. It grows out of honor, respect and trust. When a person is manipulated, intimidated or otherwise forced into submission it is not submission but subjugation.

Sexual Abuse

For a long time, it was believed that there was no such thing as sexual abuse in marriage. The husband had a "right" to the sexual attention of his wife, even when he used force.

Recently, society has come to realize that forcing one's partner to perform sexual acts that are unwanted, distasteful, or painful is abusive.

Sex with any person who is too young to understand the consequences or whose mental or emotional state keeps him/her from making an intelligent, rational decision is also abusive.

Sex with minors or the mentally handicapped is both illegal and morally wrong.

A Universal Problem

The practice of profiling, stereotyping and categorizing people does not work when it comes to domestic abuse. In America people are fond of blaming all of society's problems on a single group, namely, poor, young, inner city minorities.

Abusers are black, white, brown, olive red and yellow. They are rich, poor and everything in between. They live in tiny urban apartments, spacious suburban condominiums, gated mansions and quaint farmhouses. They are factory workers, CEOs, policemen and preachers. In short domestic abuse is a problem that crosses all possible lines of socio-economic and ethnic demarcation.

Abuse even crosses gender barriers. Overwhelmingly, men direct domestic abuse at women. However, the opposite also occurs. One Sunday afternoon, after ministering at a church in my community, I was approached by a woman who confessed that she had been in an abusive relationship but it was she, not her husband who had been the abuser.

Law enforcement reports yield some alarming facts about this issue.

- 60 per cent of all female homicide victims are known to have been killed by their husbands, former husbands or boyfriends.
- 3 per cent of male homicide victims are known to have been killed by their wives, former wives or girlfriends.
- 70 per cent of child abuse is committed by the man of the house

- Last year, over 4 million domestic assaults were reported, 20 per cent of these resulted in serious injury.
- 50 - 70 per cent of men who abuse their wives also abuse their children.
- 80 per cent of murderers and serious injuries occur when the victim attempts to escape.

Domestic abuse and violence against women is a well-documented part of our history. It is found in every society and in every age.

Many of the great female martyrs and saints were women who fought against this evil. St. Agnes of Thirteen, for example, preferred death to loosing her virginity. She was martyred by being stabbed in the neck.

St Maria Gorette resisted an attempted rape and was stabbed to death for her impertinence. She is honored because she preferred death to defilement.

St. Monica serves as the perfect example of a battered wife. She overcame an abusive husband's violent temper through patience and loving-kindness.

In the 16th century, American and European families became increasingly patriarchal. During this time, men were given increased legal control over their wives and children. Laws were enacted that severely limited women's freedom and their role in society.

Men were legally allowed to use a variety of prescribed punishments to keep their wives "in their places." The "scolds bridle," for example, was a metal cage which was placed over the head of a woman. The woman was then forced to stick out her tongue. When the cage was closed, metal spikes would be driven through the woman's tongue. The punishment was aimed at teaching the woman never to "scold" her husband.

For most of recorded history, the most highly respected herbalist have been women. Women have served their communities as midwives and healers. In fact, many women earned money and supported themselves by the practice of these occupations.

As 16th century society became more and more male dominated, the self-appointed male medical establishment took these jobs away from women. The emerging medical profession had laws passed requiring any person involved in the healing arts to be licensed. Then, they refused to grant licenses to women. Any woman who dared to protest was quickly branded a witch or a shrew.

Long before Arabs and Europeans began targeting the African for slavery. They were already merchandising their own wives and children. The "Coverture Laws" made a man legally responsible for the debts of his wife and children. The husband was said to "cover" those in his household. These laws also reduced the status of women and children to that of mere property. Thus, they were bought, sold and traded as if they were livestock. It was not at all unusual for a wife or child to be placed into indentured servitude or sold into slavery in exchange for a piece of land or to pay off a gambling debt.

2

The Saga Continues

During the middle ages, European society began to blend the persecution of women and Jews together. For example, one myth that was circulated was, "Jewish men menstruated." It was also said that Jews and women were able to turn themselves into animals. Jewish women were said to have sex with the devil and give birth to beasts. Violent storms and plagues were said to be caused by Jews or women. It is estimated that over 100,000 people were put to death as witches during this period in history. 85 per cent of these were women. The other 15 per cent were men who were believed to be related to witches.

Single women were easy targets for witch hunters because they had no husbands or sons to protect them. Some witch hunters would level unfounded charges and use them to justify stealing a woman's property and wealth. The tragic thing about all this is that the people who did such things did them in the name of God. A 16th century book on "How To Hunt Witches" closes with a prayer thanking God for "preserving the male sex from so great a crime as being a witch."

In America, laws protecting women from abuse began to be enacted after the Civil War. The first such laws appeared on the books in 1878. Many of the states would not begin enforcing these laws for another fifty years. In fact, the popular expression, "the rule of thumb" goes back to the old laws that allowed a man to beat his wife as long as the stick he used was no thicker than his thumb.

The last twenty years have brought about many changes. However, domestic abuse continues to be a widespread problem even in the industrialized, technologically advanced west. Modern laws are just now beginning to catch up with the ancient teachings of the Scriptures that all people are made in the image of God and are, therefore, worthy of just, fair and equal treatment.

There is much ado about the progress made in recent years. When it comes to technology, there is much to celebrate. It once took my mother hours to prepare the family meal. Today, it only takes a few minutes, thanks to modern technology.

Once, one had to write a letter by hand, put a stamp on it and wait several days for it to be delivered. From mailing the letter to receiving a reply could easily be a week or more. Thanks to email and text messaging, we can send a message half way around the world in seconds.

There have been many social changes as well. In the western part of the world, many of the old taboos have fallen. Some tout this as an age of social revolution and advancement, yet not all things have kept pace. Remnants of the old pre-modern era ideas about domestic abuse continue to linger.

In early America, with few exceptions, women had to be under the jurisdiction of a man. A colonial woman could not own property, vote, get a divorce or even travel safely.

Many of the colonies had laws that imposed fines on unmarried women and placed them under the supervision of male relatives or the town leaders. A single woman could not live alone; by law, she was forced to live either with her own family or another family in town.

A woman had no legal identity of her own, under the English "Coverture" system. All that she was and all that she had was vested in her husband. For this reason, it was vitally important for a woman to marry. This notion was brought to "the new world." It was all but impossible for a woman to earn a living and support herself. As far as polite society was concerned, the only place for an unmarried adult woman was in a convent.

In our, so-called, progressive age, we see subtle and not so subtle remnants of these old attitudes. There is still more social pressure on women to marry than there is on men. This is especially true in some Christian circles.

Single women are considered a threat; insecure married women look upon them as potential husband stealers. As far as some Christian leaders are concerned a woman's only place in ministry is the choir, the usher board, prayer group, the nursery or the church kitchen.

While there are laws against sex discrimination, the "old boys network" really does exist. With few exceptions women continue to find opportunities for advancement and promotion, above the middle management level, few and far between.

We continue to see reports on Television and read articles in the newspapers about the abuse and harassment of women in the work place. There are still many women across the country and around the world who feel they must endure all manner of sexual mistreatment in order to get or keep a job.

One of the reasons why the abuse of women has been tolerated so long is because many people see women as the cause of the world's problems. "We wouldn't be in the fix we are in," they say, "if poor helpless Adam had not been seduced by evil Eve, who made him eat the forbidden fruit."

It is this kind of mindless twisting of God's word that has contributed to the silence of the church when it comes to domestic abuse. Until very recently, there was very little, if anything, said about this problem from our pulpits. In fact, the church has often been guilty of sweeping these kinds of things under the rug.

I have spoken to dozens of women over the years; who tell of being beaten by husbands who are deacons, preachers and officers in the church. Most of these women do not tell anyone. In some cases, the abuse goes on for years, because the victim doesn't want to do or say anything that may damage their spouse's reputation.

In the few cases that are taken to church leaders, the response is often to blame the victim in order to protect a spouse who is in the ministry, or spare the church any embarrassment that may be caused if the problem became public knowledge.

Some time ago, I interviewed a woman on my weekly radio program who reported being sexually abused by a pastor when she was a little child; and another who's pastor repeatedly counseled her to stay in an abusive marriage in order to protect the reputation of her husband who was a minister in the same church.

During the praise service in a church, in my home state of Michigan, a twelve year old girl came under conviction and confessed that she had been having sex with her father, a popular pastor and evangelist, for over a year.

1 Peter 4:17 says, *"For the time is come that judgment must begin at the house of God..."* It is time for the violence and abuse to stop, and it is time for the church to insist upon it!

The stresses of everyday life are often used as an excuse for violence. Some men, it is said, don't know how to feel any emotion but anger. When angered, they lash out at those closest to them. I am not a psychologist; I do not claim to know what makes people tick. I am a child of God, who knows right from wrong. I know that violence is wrong. Violence is not the answer. The answer is Christ.

3

Childhood Tears and Fears

Witnessing the abuse my mother endured had a devastating impact upon my life. I fully understand why many mental health professionals and social workers consider making children witness the abuse of a loved one, a form of child abuse, in and of itself. I suffered, tremendously, as a result of the abuse and violence I was forced to witness in my home.

I was born in Memphis, Tennessee to an unwed mother. In those days, getting pregnant out of wedlock was a social taboo. A young girl in her teens who had a baby could find herself with little support, few friends and fewer options.

My grandmother helped as much as she could, but things were still very difficult. When I was about three years old, my mother decided to leave Tennessee and start a new life in Michigan. We moved to the city of Inkster, just south of Detroit. There, my mother, anxious for a new start and a better life, rushed into a marriage to a man she knew very little about. She thought he was just a social drinker. It turns out that his drinking problem was much worse than she thought.

Getting to know someone takes time. It is never wise to rush into marriage. I advise the young men and women in our church to take the time to get to know a person. Go to dinner, attend the theater, visit museums, date for a while and by all means go through a pre-marital counseling program with a competent Christian counselor or pastor.

Over the years, I've counseled a number of women whose marital problems can be traced to the fact that they rushed into marriage. The end result was, of course disappointment and in some cases divorce. Divorce is not the will of God, but neither is living in an abusive, violent marriage. The Bible says...

> *For the Lord the God of Israel says: I hate divorce and marital separation, and him who covers his garment [his wife] with violence. Therefore keep a watch upon your spirit [that it may be controlled by my Spirit], that you deal not treacherously and faithlessly [with your marriage mate].*
>
> *Malachi 2:16*

God's desire is that we live Spirit controlled lives. In the context of marriage, this means that men and women should be honest, faithful and gentle in their treatment of each other.

As time went on, my mother discovered my stepfather was more than a social drinker. In fact, he had a serious drinking problem. He was what is sometimes called "a weekend alcoholic." He stayed sober long enough to hold down a job during the week, but on weekends, he drank. He drank until he was no longer in control of the alcohol; the alcohol was in control of him.

I recall one evening when my stepfather came home intoxicated. He came in making threats and calling my mother names. He seemed to get angrier and angrier by the minute. In no time, the verbal abuse turned physical.

He was standing between my mother and the front door. She could not get out of the apartment, so she ran into the bedroom. She got down on the floor and scurried under the bed.

When my stepfather came after her, she curled up as close to the wall as she possibly could, crying and pleading for him to stop. He groped beneath the bed with one hand, trying to get hold of an arm or leg, or even her hair.

When he could not reach her, he went into the kitchen and returned with his empty beer bottles. Cussing and yelling threats, he bent over and began throwing beer bottles under the bed, trying to hit her. My mother cried out in pain and terror as the bottles came rolling and bouncing in her direction.

I watched in horror. I could not move. It was as if my feet were nailed to the floor. I could only scream and cry as I watched. I can't recall how much time passed, but the police came rushing into the small apartment. Thanks be to God, one of our neighbors had heard the commotion and called the authorities.

As I look back on the incident, I thank God for His protection. My mother could have been seriously hurt. My stepfather was so out of control that he may have even turned on me. Had it not been for the grace of God and a neighbor who cared enough to get involved, my stepfather's rage could have resulted in my mother, me or both of us being injured or even killed.

I believe, however, that God spared my mother for my sake, and he spared me because he had a plan and purpose for my life.

God has a plan for every life. Jeremiah 29:11 says, *"For I know the thoughts and plans that I have for you, says the Lord, thoughts and plans for welfare and peace, and not for evil, to give you hope in your final outcome."*

God's plan is that we should be conformed to the image of Christ, and that we should serve Him by serving humanity.

The devil is out to do whatever he can to thwart the plan of God. But, thanks be to God, the angels of the Lord, are on guard watching over us to deliver us out of the hand of the enemy (Psalm 34:7).

Unfortunately, that had not been the first incident of violence, nor would it be the last that I would witness as a child. In fact, there was a disturbing pattern. My stepfather would get drunk. Something would set him off; he would beat and abuse my mother. She would leave him for a day, a week or maybe a month or two. He would apologize and promise to change. She would go back to him and appear to be happy, until his next explosion.

When Children Witness Violence

This was a very unhealthy environment for a child. A child living in an abusive environment may experience feelings of worry, fear and nervousness. I recall being nervous and afraid much of the time. I was afraid my mother would be badly hurt.

Any time my stepfather spoke in angry tone I became very agitated and excited. My heart would race and a cloud of fear would settle over me. I knew that, in my house, a minor argument could escalate into a violent fight at any time especially if my stepfather had been drinking.

Children growing up in a home where there is abuse and violence will, undoubtedly, have the same kinds of fears. The child will fear for the health and safety of one of both parents. This will spread into other areas of the child's life, leading to bondage to a spirit of fear.

Children will sometimes be reluctant to go to school because they fear their parents will fight while they are away. When they do go to school, they are likely to have problems concentrating in class or they may act out and become unruly. Some will mimic the violent behavior modeled for them at home by name calling and hitting their classmates.

Social scientists tell us that more likely than not, children who grow up watching the significant adults in their lives use drugs or alcohol will grow up to imitate the same behavior. Statistics prove that abused children and children who grow up witnessing the abuse of a parent will likely become abusers themselves. This phenomenon will be discussed in greater detail later in this book when we deal with generational curses.

Children who live in an environment where they witness abuse and violence on a regular basis will often grow up with hearts full of anger, bitterness, and even resentment and hatred for the abuser.

I don't remember harboring any feelings of hatred toward my stepfather, but I was never able to be very close to him. I had more fear of him than respect for him. I was never sassy, impolite or disobedient, but I had no desire to embrace him as a father.

My two brothers and two sisters did not seem to be effected by the violence in our household to the same degree that I was. This may be because they were too young to be aware of what was happening and too young to be aware of the possible consequences; or maybe it was because they had been born into this environment and did not know anything else. For me, however, these episodes of anger and violence were terrifying.

My friends looked forward to the weekends. They talked about being able to stay up late because there was no school on Saturday and Sunday. There would be more time for talking on the telephone, riding bikes through the neighborhood and playing with the other kids on the block. I dreaded weekends. I knew my stepfather would celebrate making it through another week at the brick yard, with his usual drink; followed by another, then another and as many as it took for him to get drunk.

On a good week, he would just pass out and sleep it off. But if my mother said "the wrong thing," or did not do "the right thing," or if one of his drunken buddies looked at her too long or too hard, there would be trouble.

By the time I was about eight years old we had moved from the tiny apartment to a small but very nice house on the north side of Detroit. One night as my stepfather was "relaxing" with his weekend beer, I became very frightened. I don't remember what set him off. I simply remember him calling my mother names then flying into a rage like some kind of mad man.

Fearing another beating, my mother suddenly broke for the door and ran out of the house. She ran down the block crying and screaming. Horrified, I scrambled out the door, off the front porch and down the sidewalk behind her as fast as my little legs could carry me.

We ran until my mother spotted an open garage. Praying that my stepfather would not be able to find us, we ran through the neighbor's back yard and crouched there in the corner of the dark garage.

After a few minutes, the neighbor came out. She took my mother and me into her house and called the police.

As a result of the on going verbal and physical abuse, my mother suffered both emotionally and physically. She became such a nervous wreck that she could not function day to day without medication. She often complained of headaches that felt as if her skull was being squeezed in a vise. The muscles in her neck and shoulders would seize up so that her head could not rotate on her shoulders without a great deal of effort and discomfort. She sometimes had to move her entire torso in order to look to the right or to the left.

Living in fear constantly took an obvious toll on her mental and physical health. She was on one type of medication or another most of her adult life.

My mother was a licensed cosmetologist, but she could not work because of the continual stress, tension and anxiety. She managed to care for my siblings and me, but other than that, it was nearly impossible for her to lead a productive life.

Women, and in rare cases, men, pay an enormous price for the privilege of being tormented, belittled, criticized and beaten.

4

Emotional Hang Ups

Whenever I am called upon to minister in a conference or a church service, I like to take the time to pray for those in need. In doing so, over the years, I've noticed that many people suffer from guilt and shame connected to their pasts. Psalm 32.5 says...

> *I acknowledged my sin to You, and my iniquity I did not hide, I said, I will confess my transgressions to the Lord [continually unfolding the past till all is told], then You [instantly] forgave me the guilt and iniquity of my sin. Selah [pause, and calmly think of that]!*

When we come to God, in honest, sincere confession and repentance, all our past sins are forgiven instantly! In spite of the boundless mercy and endless grace of our Lord, some people continue to carry guilt and shame. This bondage to the past manifests in the form of "emotional hang-ups."

Guilt and shame about things we've done or things we've suffered in the past is unnecessary baggage. If allowed to do so, it will rob a person of the bright, happy and prosperous future he or she could have in Christ.

Keeping people bound to a troublesome past is a trick of the enemy. The enemy likes to deceive people into believing their lives are ruined forever because of things that happened in the past.

The devil is also good at getting victims to believe lies about themselves. For instance, he'll say "You are less valuable, as a person, than others. Why else would God allow this to happen to you?"

This is especially true of women and sometimes men, who have a history of bouncing from one bad relationship to another, time and time again. Satan will say, "See, no one will stay with you. You're not good enough to stay in a relationship."

One's destiny is largely shaped by his or her moral and spiritual condition. Hell is the eternal destination of those who live outside of Christ. Those who are in Christ are destined to be conformed to His image. This means that when a person comes to Christ, his entire future changes. His destiny is no longer tied to the man he was before salvation. His destiny is now tied to the new creation he has become in Christ Jesus. No matter what your life was like before you came to Christ, there are blessings in your future, now that you are in Him!

Unfortunately, many people carry anger toward the person who hurt them for years after they are no longer in the abusive situation. Some see what happened to them as God's fault and are angry with God. Since the perpetrator is no longer a part of their life and because they cannot make a fist and hit God, this anger is manifest in the way they react to and interact with the people around them. Sometimes they sabotage new friendships, because of anger and bitterness over the abuse suffered in past relationships.

This kind of anger is unhealthy. It makes a person difficult to get along with and unpleasant to be around. Not only does it hinder the development of meaningful friendships, it puts off the opposite sex, and may actually have a negative impact upon one's career and family life. Generally, people try to avoid negative individuals.

There are many men and women who attempt to cover their pain and protect themselves from more hurt, by putting up a tough facade. They pretend that nothing and no one can get to them. They deliberately keep everyone at a safe emotional distance by acting "hard core," as my teen-aged daughter would say.

Such a person will strut, and snort like an angry bull, in truth, he is in pain. Often, such people appear to be strong, assertive and even aggressive. In truth, they are really trying to hide their vulnerability. They have few, if any, real friends because people don't like being around them any more than necessary. They like to appear icy and cold, unmoved by anything human or divine. For all their bluster, they are really people in need of healing and deliverance. The writer of the book of Hebrews warns that bitterness and hostility can cause all kinds of problems and may lead to sin.

> *Exercise foresight and be on the watch to look [after one another], to see that no one falls back from hand fails to secure God's grace (His unmerited favor and spiritual blessing), in order that no root of resentment (rancor, bitterness or hatred) shoot forth and cause trouble and biter torment, and the many become contaminated and defiled by it.*
> *Hebrews 12:15*

If you have been abused, you must seek God for complete healing. This not only means healing any physical scars, but the healing of any and all emotional scars as well.

I believe some people today are ill, suffering with emotional and physical problems because of unhealthy emotions. Some people suffer from sickness such as arthritis, anxiety and other emotional and mental disorders because they have allowed a root of bitterness to spring up in their souls.

Those who jump in and out of one bad, exploitive relationship after another are usually desperate for love or anything that will salve the wounds of past abuse. I see so many women who after being hurt leave the bad relationship, only to get involved in another where she is eventually hurt again. This pattern is devastating to a person's spiritual and emotional welfare.

I'm not sure how it is that Mary Magdalene came to be possessed of "seven" demons, could it be the result of her repeated involvement with men who only took her body and left her feeling unloved and rejected.

The Spirit of Jezebel

Some abuse victims become very controlling and manipulative. It starts out as a defense mechanism. During the time in their lives when they were being abused they felt powerless. Some one else had control. The result of someone else being in control was abuse, mistreatment and violence. To insure nothing like that happens to them again. They determine to take control, themselves.

I must say, there is nothing wrong with deciding to no longer live under the domination and control of an abusive spouse. In fact, this is an admirable thing. It is something else, altogether, when a person claims to be taking control of his life, but is operating out of fear, anger and hurt. When this is the case that person is really surrendering control to the devil.

The person operating out of unhealthy emotions will not surrender to the Holy Spirit's control, but feels that he or she must, themselves, be in control. This person fears that allowing anyone, including God, to be in control may result in more hurt. This is a mindset that demons love to exploit. The devil will deceive such a person into believing that in order to be in control of his or her own life, he or she must control everything around them, including other people.

To gain and maintain control this person will go to almost any length, including lies, manipulation and trickery.

Often this individual comes under the influence of the spirit of Jezebel. Jezebel is an evil spirit from Satan that causes both men and women to distrust and hate anyone they cannot control. A woman operating in the spirit of Jezebel will not have a relationship with a man who does not have an Ahabish mentality. She will not tolerate a man who is not weak, gullible and easy to control. The Jezebelic woman has a secret hatred for strong men. If given the chance, she will destroy his strength and destroy his life.

Both men and women who operate in the spirit of Jezebel have a special hatred for the men and women of God. The ministers of the Lord are controlled by the Holy Spirit and not open to control by men. For this reason, Jezebel hates them and seeks opportunities to undermine them and bring them down.

If we could look into the spirit realm we would discover that in the overwhelming majority of cases where a man or woman of God falls into the kind of sin that destroys his or her reputation, compromises ministry and robs them of the anointing, the spirit of Jezebel is involved.

A woman operating in the spirit of Jezebel may seduce the man of God. She will lure him into sexual sin, then, use his fear of exposure to control both the man and his ministry.

If she is married, you can rest assured that the Jezebelic woman is married to a man who hates conflict and confrontation. He is usually easy going and, more, importantly, easily manipulated. If a man is not of that disposition at the start, Jezebel will work to bring him to that place. She will often employ her favorite weapon, sex, as a means of accomplishing this. For Jezebel, sex is not an expression of love, but a bargaining chip. Her spouse's sexual needs are to be exploited. Sex is given in exchange for control.

Most Jezebelic men, have a problem with authority, especially spiritual authority. They are difficult men to deal with in the church. They want to be the power behind the pulpit, so to speak. They want to control the church by controlling its leadership. The man operating in the spirit of Jezebel usually chooses money as his weapon. Being master manipulators, the Jezebelic male will often work under cover to organize financial rebellions in the House of God. He will corner people in the lobby and in the church parking lot and convince them to stop supporting the ministry and the leadership financially. His hope is that when church leaders realize how influential he is, they will abdicate their responsibility. He usually does not want the leadership to step down. He is happy for them to remain as window dressing, while he controls the church from behind the scenes. Many church splits have been caused by folk operating in the spirit of Jezebel.

Leaders who do not believe that God can provide for the church will compromise, but compromise with Jezebel will lead to the collapse of the ministry. The money may flow again, but the power of God will not. When church leaders compromise with Jezebel, you can change the name of the church to "Icabod," because the glory of the Lord will leave.

In such cases, one must fault both the individual who allowed the devil to use him and the leader who allowed himself to be manipulated.

When the person operating in the spirit of Jezebel is the victim of past abuse our hearts go out to them. A heart of compassion is a part of the pastoral anointing. However, church leaders cannot be so compassionate that we fail to correct when correction is needed. The enemy will exploit this kind of "sloppy agape." The Jezebelic spirit will play on our sympathies to get his or her way, this tactic is more palatable, but its results are no less disastrous.

Sexual Promiscuity

Sexual promiscuity is another "hang-up" or emotional problem often seen in the victims of abuse. Contrary, to what some might believe, promiscuity is not always caused by an overwhelming appetite for sex, nor an unusually high sex drive. In many cases, people who sleep around are really looking for tenderness, love and affection. When this longing is not satisfied in one relationship, they look for it in another, and then another. This is especially true of victims of incest and childhood sexual abuse. As mentioned earlier, most men who abuse their wives also abuse their children.

One of my most painful and embarrassing moments came when I was 12 years old, just months before I became a Christian. I'm somewhat reluctant to put it in this book. I don't want my brothers and sisters to feel that I am besmirching the memory of their father. On the other hand, I'm compelled; by the Holy Spirit, to tell the whole story so that others may be blessed.

My mother questioned me one day about my stepfather's behavior toward me. He was such a vile man that she thought him capable of anything. She suspected he had been molesting me. When I denied it, she took me to the pastor's house and the pastor and his wife question me. My mother believed that I would be afraid to lie to the man and woman of God and her suspicions would be confirmed.

I was so embarrassed and afraid that I really could not think clearly, I certainly was not about to say "yes." Instead, I denied it to the very end.

The truth is, my stepfather never tried to penetrate me, as far as I can remember, but I do remember that when I was very small, he had fondled me. I continued to hide the molestation until well into adulthood. I never spoke about it to anyone not to my mother, and not to my husband until I began writing this book.

People, who are sexually molested as children, often grow up to have extreme views of sex. Some homosexual's and lesbians tell of being molested by members of the same sex as children. Some victims grow up to be frigid and sexually unavailable, even in marriage. Others grow up to equate sex with love.

Sex, is not love. Within the context of marriage, sex is an expression of love. It is one of several ways that love is communicated; but sex is not love nor is it an adequate substitute for love.

If it had not been for my grandmother, Irene, who took me to church and led me to the Lord, when I was twelve years old, my life could have been very different. I could have been sexually promiscuous. The door to bondage in that area had certainly been opened by what my stepfather had done. But as I grew in the Lord, through my teens, I was kept from sexual sin by my commitment to Christ, my grandmother's encouragement and the power of the Holy Spirit.

I have seen the result of promiscuity, time and time again. A promiscuous lifestyle opens one up to all manner of physical and emotional sickness. At best it is a hollow life, one that only brings on more disappointment and pain. At worse, one may contract any one of a number of incurable diseases such as Herpes or HIV and die prematurely.

Depression

Some counselors believe that abuse in childhood can result in depression later in life. This is borne out by both statistics and my experience with abuse survivors.

Because the abuse took place when they were very young, small in size and defenseless, many victims have feelings of helplessness that follow them into adulthood. When coupled with anger, resentment, hurt and guilt, these lead to negative thinking and depression.

Depression can be so debilitating that persons suffering from it can find that they have trouble functioning day to day. They are sad nearly all the time. In severe cases they find it hard to hold down a job, maintain meaningful relationships or perform simple daily tasks.

A person suffering from depression may neglect his personal hygiene and health. He or she may be seen going about with uncombed hair and dirty clothes. If a depressed person has children, they too are often unkempt and neglected.

Depressed people often lack self-confidence, so they retreat into a world of fantasy; preferring to spend their time day dreaming and pretending to be their favorite TV or movie hero, rather than in productive pursuits.

Hypochondria, sexual promiscuity, gambling, substance abuse, work-a-holism, and angry outbursts are all signs that a person may be trying to hide a serious case of depression.

Children, especially, will try to hide their hurt by acting out in disturbing ways. Many teen-aged run-aways are children trying to escape the throes of a seemingly unbearable depression. When people realize they cannot run from their internal torments, they often turn to thoughts of suicide.

Pride

Proverbs 16: 18, says, *"Pride goes before destruction and a haughty spirit before a fall."* Of all human emotions, pride is the one singled out in the Bible as the most destructive.

Pride is one of the most reliable predictors of trouble known to man. According to the writer of the proverb, when one becomes proud, heady, high minded and haughty, you can be assured that, it is just a matter of time before he or she falls and stumbles into ruin.

Many victims of abuse suffer from low self-esteem, guilt and shame. Rather than turning to Christ, who is able to heal these unhealthy emotions, they attempt to cover them with pride.

Many haughty people are not people who see themselves as better than everyone else. They, in fact, may be suffering from self-doubt and low self-esteem but want the world to see them as superior. They are often afraid that people will peer into their souls, see that they are no good, and dislike them or they fear that people will see them as weak and vulnerable and they will be victimized again. Their pride is an attempt to hide these feelings behind a front of superciliousness. The enemy exploits their unhealthy emotions, influencing them to become conceited, smug and vain as a defense.

The problem is whenever we try to cover flesh with flesh we always go overboard. It is like the drunk man, who, upon realizing that he is about to fall to the left abruptly shifts his weight to the right to compensate, only to realize that now he is in danger of falling to the other side.

The victim of abuse, to keep from falling into the pit of despair on the left, shifts too much and falls into pride on the right. The bitterness and anger at what they have gone through, coupled with fear of ever going through it again leads them to put on a mask that says, "You can't touch me...I am better than you."

Ruin comes when, because of their haughty and superficial personality, people grow to dislike them, and turn away from them. When such a person claims to be a Christian, he or she will have a tendency toward self-importance and self-exaltation. He or she will insist upon operating in a ministry calling they are obviously not anointed to. They will often crave positions of leadership and influence or positions that get a great deal of public notice. They despise correction and may become quite a disruptive force in the assembly.

Their anger and bitterness may open them up to the influence of the Jezebel spirit. They may even attempt to entice church leaders into inappropriate relationships, thinking, "See, I must be special; even the pastor wants me." If the abuse they suffered was sexual, they may be unable to receive love from heart to heart. Confused, they think sex is the only expression of love, so they fall into promiscuity.

Hebrews 12:16 warns that bitterness, growing out of unhealthy emotions can cause one to fall into "*sexual vice, or become a profane (godless and sacrilegious) person as Esau did, who sold his own birthright for a single meal* [Genesis 25:29-34].

Anger

Anger is often at the heart of the emotional hang-ups that abuse victims suffer. Noted Christian psychologist and author Gary Collins, points out, in his book, *Christian Counseling: A Comprehensive Guide,* that anger may come from any one of a number of sources.

(1) Anger may come from *"injustice."* One of the things that raised the fury of the nation concerning the September 11 attacks, was the injustice of it all. No matter how one views the crisis in the Middle East and the Palestinian situation, all rational human beings see an attack upon innocent people as an abominable injustice.

(2) Anger may also come from *"threat and hurt."* According to Collins, "when a person is rejected, put down, humiliated, unjustly criticized or otherwise threatened, anger is often aroused."

With victims of domestic violence and abuse, this anger can be either turned outward, toward the abuser, or it may be suppressed and turned inward. Suppressed anger cannot remain suppressed forever. From time to time, it will surface, as anger directed at people; people who may not have had anything to do with what the victims suffering.

Many survivors of abuse live behind a wall of anger, and refuse to allow anyone to get close enough to hurt them again. Unfortunately, this wall also keeps out those who care and want to help.

(3) Anger can also be *"a learned response."* This is especially true of children who witness abuse. These children, by observation, learn that angry, aggressive behavior is the way to get what they want. They grow up using anger as a means of manipulating people and imposing their will on others.

Victims turn their anger inward because they are afraid that if they express any anger, the abuse will only get worse; so they suppress their anger. Suppressed anger gives birth to feelings of worry, fear, stress and tension. It may manifest in the form of physical illness; headaches, ulcers and high blood pressure, for example. Suppressed anger can also lead to thoughts of suicide, murder or both.

Loneliness

Many victims of abuse feel as if they are all alone. As stated earlier, isolation is often a tactic used by abusers. They cut off communication between the victim and his or her family and close friends. They monitor the victim's comings and goings. Some abusers have been known to remove the telephones from the house or remove the battery from the family car so that the victim will be cut off from all help and support.

Eventually, the victim begins to feel that he or she is totally alone. "No one knows what I'm going through and no one cares," becomes the victims prevailing sentiment. The abuser may even pound that notion into the victim's head. "No body cares about you...no body is going to help you...no one wants you...you're nothing...who do you think will listen to you!"

The isolation plus low self-esteem caused by constant put downs, equals feelings of loneliness on the part of the victim. Lonely people have trouble relating to others, as a result, they may lash out angrily, or become self-centered. These, of course only push people away and lead to even further isolation. Extreme loneliness can lead to feelings of hopelessness and despair.

Un healthy emotions must never be nurtured. The more they are fed, the more they grow. Eventually unhealthy emotions become character flaws. Character flaws make people easy targets for the enemy. It is the flaws and weaknesses in the human character that Satan seeks to exploit and use to torment, harass and oppress.

There is good news, however. Jesus can heal and deliver and make you free from unhealthy emotions

> *Come to Me, all you who labor and are heavy-laden and over burdened, and I will cause you to rest-I will ease and relieve and refresh your souls. Take My yoke upon you, and learn of Me; for I am gentle (meek) and humble (lowly) in heart, and you will find rest-relief, ease and refreshment and recreation and blessed quiet for your souls.*
>
> Matthew 11:28,29

5

Stop Blaming Yourself

Many victims actually blame themselves. They say, "Its my fault." This is common in victims of childhood molestation, incest and rape. Many victims are made to feel that something they said, something they did, or something about the way they look caused them to be targeted by their abusers.

A woman who has been raped may blame herself for looking too provocative. She may ask herself, "What did I do?" Was my dress too short? Was my blouse cut too low" Did I do something to turn him on?"

Any one or all of these things may or may not be true. In the final analysis, however, these are really not the issue. The abuser knows right from wrong, and he alone is responsible for the choice to victimize another human being.

Let's be honest, it is foolish to intentionally, flirt in the presence of a jealous spouse. To do so is to invite trouble. To deliberately dress in a sexually provocative manner violates God's Word concerning modesty and moderation. It invites lustful attention.

I agree that a man or a woman has the right to wear whatever he or she chooses. But let us not be naive, our choices have consequences. It is simply not wise to knowingly make a choice whose consequences we are not prepared to deal with; and let's not forget that rights are violated every day. I'm not sure that crying..."its my right," after the deed is done will do much to help heal the scars. Even if the perpetrator is arrested and jailed, the victim must still deal with the damage done to his or her life. Yes, it is my right, but I wouldn't play near and open flame wearing a paper dress.

Having said that, however, I must also say, "two wrongs don't make a right." The actions of the victim don't excuse the sins of the perpetrator. Every person has a choice. He may respond in a proper and acceptable manner, or he may do that which is evil.

A man may walk away from that provocatively dressed woman, or he may choose to violate her and abuse her. He must make the choice; and he alone is responsible for the choice he makes.

Violence, rape and abuse are never about sex and seldom do strangers perpetrate these acts. People are most likely to be victimized by someone they know. In fact, someone with whom the victim has had a close personal relationship commits most crimes against one's person.

These sinful acts are about anger, rage and control. They are about humiliating the victim and forcing him or her into compliance with the perpetrators, often unreasonable and ungodly demands.

Don't buy the, "I couldn't help myself," or the "See what you made me do," argument; don't blame yourself. The temptation to blame oneself is often rooted in some other past trauma. The failure to properly understand some event from the past can trigger self-blaming. Children, who were abandoned, may not understand why they were unwanted. They think, "I must be bad, or mom or dad would not have left.

If you, yourself are a child of divorce, or if one of your parents died when you were very young, you may have subconsciously blamed yourself. This gives way to a spirit of self-blaming that causes you to blame yourself whenever things go wrong. Even when matters are completely out of your control, somehow, you see yourself as the reason for all disappointments and difficulties. You will even blame yourself when other people mistreat and abuse you.

Self-blaming may be made worse by family, friends and sometimes professionals (police, counselors, clergy and etc.) who lack a clear understanding of the real issues involved in domestic violence and abuse. Untrained professionals may suggest the abuse will stop if you change your behavior or your attitude.

Sometimes, self-blaming is an unconscious attempt to gain some kind of power in a situation in which, you are otherwise powerless. It comes out of the sense that, "If I change, the abuse will change." the truth is, you have no power to change another person. The abuser is dealing with his own issues. There is nothing you can do or say to change him. You can only pray that someday, he will have the desire to seek the Lord and allow God to save him and change him. Until that time, you need to recognize that there is a problem and take steps to get out.

Just think about it. Should the bank robber be excused because he could not help it; there was just so much money in that bank? What about the car thief who would not have stolen that car if it had not had such a great custom paint job?

No matter what the temptation, the abuser made the choice to abuse. He alone, not the victim, is responsible for his diabolic acts.

"I couldn't help it...you made me do it...I love you so much, that I go crazy" These are all lies aimed at shifting responsibility from the perpetuator to the victim. No one is ever to be blamed for the evil acts visited upon them by someone else. The abuser and the abuser alone is responsible for the evil he has done.

6

Receive Your Healing

Abuse of any kind can have a devastating impact upon an individual's life, but there is good news. There is healing and hope in Jesus Christ.

Hundreds of years before Jesus was born in Bethlehem, the Prophet Isaiah spoke of His ministry to the poor, the suffering and, yes, the abused.

> *He was despised and rejected and forsaken by men, a Man of sorrows and pains, and acquainted with grief and sickness; and like one from whom men hide their faces He was despised, and we did not appreciate His worth or have any esteem for Him. Surely He has borne our griefs (sicknesses, weaknesses, and distresses) and carried our sorrows and pains [of punishment], yet we [ignorantly] considered Him stricken, smitten, and afflicted by God [as if with leprosy] [Matthew 8:17]. But He was wounded for our transgressions, He was bruised for our guilt and iniquities; the chastisement [needful to obtain] peace and well being for us was upon Him, and with the stripes [that wounded] Him we are healed and made whole.*
>
> Isaiah 53:3-5

When Christ hung on the cross at Calvary, He paid the price for our healing. He suffered the cruelest form of abuse imaginable so that we may be delivered.

No matter how horrific our experiences, no matter how deep the scars, we can be healed by the power of the risen Christ.

The steps to deliverance are very simple.

Step 1: Acknowledge the Problem

The first step to deliverance is acknowledging that there is a problem. I have seen victims who deny the fact that a problem exists. These folks will go on suffering until they are able to admit that there is something wrong.

Experience has taught me that most problems don't just go away. When ignored, problems only get worse. Abuse and violence are problems that can cost a victim his or her physical and/or mental health when ignored for too long. Some have even lost their lives.

I am not one of those radical feminists that you've seen on the television talk shows pushing for a man-hating, matriarchal society. I am not trying to convince every female in the world that she is automatically a victim just because she is a woman. I realize that most of us grew up in loving homes. The only violence we ever witnessed was on television or on the city streets. Many women, and men alike, enjoy the fruits of happy, healthy marriages.

My experience was different, but not unusual. I am a woman who grew up watching her mother endure verbal abuse and beatings on a regular basis. Living with this violence day to day, traumatized me tremendously. I became a fearful, shy and nervous child.

Thanks be to God, I found deliverance and healing for my anxiety ridden mind and my battered emotions in Christ. The Lord saved me, filled me with the Holy Spirit and called me to tell other survivors that there is hope in Him.

The first step toward realizing that hope in your own life is to acknowledge that there is a problem. If you fear being hit or humiliated, if you have ever been struck during an argument, there is a problem. If you are not allowed to communicate with friends and family, if you are continually made feel as if you are nothing, there is a problem. You don't have to live with it, acknowledge it and get out and get help.

If you are a survivor of abuse, and you are still wearing the emotional scars, you too need to acknowledge it, and let the Lord God heal you and make you whole again.

Step 2: Forgive

If you are a person who has suffered any type of abuse, you need to forgive the person or persons who hurt you. You must remember your own forgiveness depends upon your willingness to forgive others.

> *And whenever you stand praying, if you have anything against anyone, forgive him and let it drop-leave it, let go-in order that your Father Who is in Heaven may also forgive you your [own] failings and shortcomings and let them drop. But if you do not forgive, neither will your Father in Heaven forgive your failings and shortcomings.*
> *Mark 11:25*

I realize this is not an easy thing for some of us to do. It can be very hard to release and let go of the hurts of the past. Our human nature wants to hold on to the anger and resentment that has built up over the years. We may even have feelings of revenge. We want the person who hurt us to feel as much, if not more, pain that we feel.

I remember something that happened when I was six or seven years old. It was one Friday evening. My stepfather was late getting home from work that night. This being the weekend, mother was sure that he had stopped off somewhere with his friends, had some drinks, and would come home intoxicated and angry. She had determined that this, Friday evening would be different. This Friday evening, she was not going to take a beating. This would be the day when the abuse would end. This would be the day that she would finally do some thing that would send the message that she was tired of the abuse and give her the satisfaction of a little revenge.

As she prepared dinner that evening, she put an extra pot of water on the stove. It was my stepfather's habit to come into the house through the back door. He would remove his work boots and leave them on the basement landing, then climb the two or three stairs that led to the kitchen.

That evening, when my mom heard him at the back door, she went into the kitchen. Picked up the pot of boiling water and waited for him to step through the kitchen door. With a sudden jerk of the arm and flick of the wrist, my mother sent steaming hot water flying in my stepfather's direction. The scalding liquid splashing into his face, it ran onto his chest, arms and legs, burning and melting flesh as it went.

My mother dropped the pot and ran out of the house. She ran to a neighbor's house and called the police, who never arrived. Mom stayed away that night, but she returned the next morning and talked him into going to the hospital.

According to Romans 12:17 we are to "Repay no one evil for evil." The victim of abuse does not need revenge; he or she needs healing. He needs to get out of the situation, get to a safe place and he needs to forgive the abuser.

Forgiveness does not mean that one must continue to put oneself at risk. Forgiveness means to no longer hold that person responsible for what he did although he is indeed guilty. This is a concept that should be easy for Christian's to understand. We have all "sinned and come short of the glory of God," yet because of Jesus Christ, God does not hold our past sin against us.

The person who hurt you is guilty. Forgiveness means that you no longer make it your business to keep an account of the wrong. Instead, you make the choice to leave it in the hands of God, while you move on with your life.

Some people are reluctant to forgive because they feel that forgiveness lets the offender off the hook. Nothing could be further from the truth. Forgiveness lets you off the hook. It keeps you from being forever tied to the person and the pain by negative memories and the emotions they evoke. You are free, and the guilty person must still answer to God.

> *Beloved, never avenge yourselves, but leave the way open for [God's] wrath; for it is written, Vengeance is mine, I will repay (requite), say the Lord.*
> *Romans 12:19*

When we forgive, it leaves the door open for our own healing, and for God to deal with the abuser.

My stepfather was a violent man. With the exception of that single incident, my mother was and is a very forgiving person. After years of abuse suffered at his hand, she loved my stepfather. They eventually separated, but my mother seldom, if ever, had any negative thing to say about him. Even after the separation she treated him with kindness. He, on the other hand, continued to be harsh, cruel and abusive in his language toward her.

My stepfather's life ended violently. One summer afternoon as he was leaving a neighborhood bar, he decided to stop at a nearby party store to purchase some beer to take home.

As he stepped back out onto the sidewalk with his purchase in hand, two men confronted him and demanded his wallet.

Being the stubborn, violent man that he was, my stepfather was not about to hand over his money without a fight. When he refused to surrender his wallet, one of the men pulled out a small caliber handgun and placed it against my stepfather's forehead between his eyebrows and pulled the trigger. The bullet tore through his brain taking gray matter with it as it exited out of the back of his head. He was pronounced "dead on arrival" at an area hospital. His thirty dollars were still in his wallet. His attackers have never been caught.

When you forgive, your feelings toward your abuser may not change at once. Forgiveness is not about feelings. It is about freedom. Forgiveness frees you to live without allowing a painful past to impact your future.

Don't worry about your feelings, simply set your will to forgive. When the will is set, the feelings will follow, in time.

In addition to forgiving the perpetrator, you may also need to forgive some other people. You may need to forgive family, friends, counselors and clergy whose lack of knowledge and understanding resulted in bad advice; advice that led to prolonged suffering and pain.

Let me share a simple prayer for forgiveness...

Heavenly Father, I thank you for showing me the way out of a terrible situation. Just as the Lord Jesus forgave those who abused him at Calvary, I forgive

any and all persons who have abused, misused, hurt and disappointed me.
Father, I release them and the pain they caused, from my Spirit and from my soul this day. I set my will to forgive and I do forgive them, in the name of Jesus. Amen.

Step 3: Seek Forgiveness for Yourself

In teaching His disciples to pray, Jesus told them to say, "...Forgive us our debts, as we forgive our debtors." You see, when we forgive, we actually, help facilitate our own forgiveness. We cut ties that keep us bound to the past and we set the stage for a future free of torment.

While it is natural to have feelings of anger, resentment and even hatred toward the people who hurt and disappoint us, it is not Christ like. While He was still on the cross, enduring the shame, anguish and pain of the crucifixion, Jesus prayed that God would forgive his abuser. Christ-likeness requires that we do the same.

In forgiving our abusers, we must also seek forgiveness for any ungodly attitudes and/or feelings that we may have held against any persons who have done us harm. We are assured of forgiveness, because of our willingness to forgive others.

If we [freely] admit that we have sinned and confess our sins He is faithful and just (true to his own nature and promises) and will forgive our sins (dismiss our lawlessness).
1 John 1:9

God promises to cleanse us from all our sin and we don't need to wait until next Sunday; you can be forgiven right now; it only takes a simple prayer, uttered in sincerity.

Heavenly Father, I confess that I have held bitterness, anger resentment and many other negative things in my heart as a result of the abuse I suffered in the past.

Father, I do not want to carry these burdens any longer. I ask You to forgive me for every ungodly thought, imagination and emotion.

Deliver me and make me free by the power of the risen Christ, in Jesus name.

Step 4: Break Generational Curses

Unhealthy emotions can be passed on to our children and our children's children. The unhealthy emotions in our lives may, in fact, have been passed on to us from our parents, grandparents or great grandparents.

As children, we my have learned these negative responses from the adults around us. By virtue of being handed down from one generation to the next, these negative, unhealthy emotions have become a curse that hinders us and will hinder our children unless the curse is broken.

There is an interesting verse in the book of Exodus.

You shall not bow down yourself to them or serve them; for I the Lord your God am a jealous God, visiting the iniquity of the fathers upon the children to the third and fourth generations of those who hate Me,

Exodus 20:5

Notice the phrase "visiting the iniquity of the fathers upon the children..." This is what is known as a generational curse.

The Prophet Jeremiah restates this same spiritual law.

> *Who shows loving-kindness to thousands, and recompenses the iniquity of the fathers into the bosom of their children after them. The great, the Mighty God, the Lord of hosts is His name*
>
> *Jeremiah 32:18*

This does not mean the children are made responsible, in the Day of Judgment, for the sins of the fathers. Every person is responsible for his own actions. However, the actions of the fathers can and do have an impact upon the lives of the children.

This truth is evident in the society around us. No better example can be seen than that provided by the criminal justice system. The overwhelming majority of those in prison come from broken homes. There are even cases in which both the fathers and the sons have been in and out of jail most of their adult lives.

It is a well-known fact that many abused children grow up to become abusers. The children learn the ungodly behavior from the fathers. Likewise, the negative consequences associated with that behavior is experienced by the children.

Without realizing it, both perpetrators and victims of abuse teach their children to follow in their footsteps. Perpetrators and victims, alike, pass on their negative behavior and unhealthy emotions to their children.

Many victims are simply repeating the behavior modeled for them by one or both of their parents. The parent who tolerates abuse over a long period of time inadvertently teaches his or her children to expect to be abused and to accept it. The person who inflicts abuse upon a spouse teaches his children that this is the way one is to deal with the disagreements that arise in marriage.

The good news is that you can be the one to break the curse and end the cycle of abuse for yourself and for your children.

Living in a home where I witnessed abuse often, I became a very nervous and fearful child. When anyone raised his or her voice or spoke in an angry tone, my heart would pound as if it was trying to leap right out of my chest. A strong spirit of fear would come over me. I could hardly speak and I would shake uncontrollably. I would suffer from shortness of breath sometimes, I would actually faint.

My mother took me to several doctors who wanted to put me on medication for anxiety. Several times prescriptions were written for me, but I refused to take the drugs.

I was about twelve years old when my grandmother came from Memphis to visit with us for the summer. My grandmother was a truly faithful Believer. Even though she was more than seven hundred miles from her home church, she attended worship every week, almost without fail. She discovered a church in the neighborhood that she liked and started taking me to services with her. As a result of the grace of God and my grandmother's prayers, I gave my life to the Lord and was filled with the Holy Spirit.

At that time, I was only twelve years old and just a babe in the Lord. I did not know anything about operating in faith. Never the less, I was moved by the Holy Spirit to steadfastly refuse to take any medication for my nerves. Even as a pre-teen aged child, I was determined that I was not going to be on medication for the rest of my life. I was determined to be healed and made free by the power of God.

It was not an instant healing. It took some time, but I continued to stand on God's Word; the little of it that I knew then. I continued to refuse to be medicated. When anxiety attacks came, I would pray and praise God. I really can't place a time and date on the moment the attacks stopped. I can only report that at some point they ceased and today I am free.

The prayer of faith breaks curses. The following is an example of a prayer for deliverance from generational curses.

> *Heavenly Father, I thank you for your boundless grace and mercy. I thank you for saving me and filling me with the Holy Spirit.*
>
> *Father, this day, in the name of Jesus, I take authority over the forces of evil that come to keep me bound. This day, I loose and free myself from any and all ancestral curses. I am not bound to repeat the sins of my fathers. I am a new creation in Christ. Old things are passed away all things are become new.*
>
> *I decree it and I receive it, in Jesus name. Amen.*

Step 5: Seek God for Deliverance

We should then ask God to deliver us from every tormenting spirit connected and/or related to the abuse. Satan is a master at exploiting suffering. He will seek to introduce ungodly thoughts and use them as an entry point into our lives and as legal grounds for persecution.

When we hold onto and nurture unhealthy emotions we open the door to bondage. Once bound, we have a very difficult time resisting the urge to express ungodly ideas and act out in ungodly ways. It seems that against our better judgment, against what we know is right we find ourselves compelled to behave according to the dictates of the ungodly emotions within. Satan will keep compelling us and goading us until he has caused us to destroy our own lives.

God is faithful; He will set us free from, anger, resentment, depression, low self-esteem and all the tormenting spirits of the enemy. By the power of the risen Christ, we will be made free from pride and every other destructive emotion. The fear and distrust of people will become a thing of the past and we will be healed from the inside out. Let me share another prayer with you, a simple prayer for deliverance.

> *Lord God, you are the Strong and Mighty One, you are the one who is mighty in battle, mighty to deliver.*
>
> *I confess that the enemy has entered my life to destroy all that is holy and good. I am tormented by spirits of anger, resentment and suicide (name all of those things that are troubling you). These things are not from you Lord; they are spirits from the enemy. Right now, I ask for deliverance from all these ungodly influences. In the name of Jesus, the Christ, I command that these and all connected and related spirits go from me.*
>
> *I thank you, Father, for making me free, in the name of Jesus. Amen.*

7

Walk In Victory

Finally, we are able to walk in victory. Finally, we are able to become the men and women God wants us to be without the tormenting bondage to things that happened to us in the past.

Healing is not always instaneous, but it is always guaranteed.

My healing began even before I was completely delivered out of that violent, abusive environment. When I accepted Christ the Holy Spirit began to lead me to refuse to accept what I was seeing in my home as the way it should be. He gave me to know that God had another plan for my life.

My mother was not a Christian in those days. She had been raised in the church and had operated in the prophetic at one time. She was seduced and drawn away from Christ by the illusion of good times in the fast lane. It led to a difficult life with an abusive man.

My grandmother, a mighty woman of God, lived in another state, seven hundred miles away, so I had little support at home. But, I was determined to have a different kind of life. I was determined to live for God. A Pastor, Elder Ezekiel White and his wife, who had no children or their own, at the time, took a special interest in me. They would pick me up for church, take me out to dinner, take me shopping; they treated me as if I were their own daughter.

When our family moved from the town of Inkster to Detroit, I was in my teens and I began looking for another church home. At the time, the nearest Pentecostal church was about one mile, perhaps a little more, from our house. I was the only Believer in my household; no one else was interested in going to church. I remember times when I would cry because I could not get anyone to take me to church. After a while, I started riding the city bus. It always seemed to run slow on Sundays. Sometimes, I would walk. I knew that if I could get there, I could always find someone to give me a ride back home.

In spite of all that was going on in my home, I was a pretty good student. The Lord blessed me to find favor with some caring teachers who encouraged me to study hard and excel in school. My grades were good so my teachers encouraged me to enroll in Cass Technical High School.

Cass was a specialty school. At the time, it was known as one of the schools in the area where the "smart kids" went.

Some of my cousins and other relatives would put me down and even physically attack me. They accused me of trying to be better than them because I refused to be drawn into their world of promiscuity, alcoholism and drug abuse. They would try to drag me to clubs and parties, but I would refuse to go. They would introduce me to guys, but I refused to be seduced by someone with nothing to offer but conversation and the opportunity to become an unwed mother. My stand for God and my own expectations of a better life angered them. They would pick on me and say things like, "You must think you're too good." I have never considered myself any better than others. I simply realized that with Jesus, I could have a better life.

I was quite shy, but I managed to always find the courage to witness for Christ. In fact, when I finally started dating, I insisted that the young men who took me out also come to church. If a young man would not attend worship with me, I would soon stop going out with him.

I credit my Christian commitment for keeping me from being victimized by young men who only wanted to exploit me sexually. I was firm and unyielding in my determination to be a virtuous woman. Fellows who were only interest in sex got the message right away and they did not stick around very long.

One day, as I was rushing through the crowded hallway at school, a friend of mine yelled out to me. From halfway up the staircase, I looked back to see her standing at her locker with a handsome young man. "Pat," she said, "this is Gregory. Gregory, this is Pat." I must say, Kathy caught me off guard; I did not quite know how to respond to the sudden, unexpected introduction. I just said "Hi," and scampered up the stairs to my next class. Well, to make a long story short, Gregory chased me around the hallways for a couple of weeks. Finally, I decided to let him catch me. I did not know it at the time, but looking back, I think it was God's plan.

Greg was interesting; he was different from most of the guys who walked the halls at school. He was kind of quiet, kind of shy but without being a nerd. In spite of his shy demeanor there was strength and a quiet confidence about him. He was not cocky, just confident in his own tranquil way.

Needless to say, we started dating and I started witnessing. I was never pushy, I simply talked about Christ whenever, what seemed to be, an appropriate opportunity presented itself; and I continued to comport myself in a manner befitting a godly woman. When I invited him to visit my church, he eagerly agreed. It turns out that his grandfather was a pastor and his grandmother was the church musician.

Heath, as I call him, was one of those people who had grown up around the church but had never accepted Christ. Eventually, however, as we continued dating, he came to a saving knowledge of Jesus Christ and accepted the call to the ministry. He and I were married a short time later.

My personal ministry began to grow when Heath was asked to accept the job of senior pastor at a small congregation about thirty miles or so from our home. Working with him, I soon came out of that shell of shyness and began to grow as a teacher and mentor to the young women of the church.

I was learning and growing but it was still unclear as to God's ultimate purpose for my life. That is, until one Sunday evening in our monthly Women's Ministry Service.

As I began to address the women and men gathered in the sanctuary, I felt an unusual anointing. I had prepared a message entitled *Abused But Not Shaken*. After about ten minutes of speaking, I began to feel the Holy Spirit tugging at my spirit. He pulled me away from my prepared outline into a different place in Him.

2 Peter 1:21 says the prophets "*spake as they were moved by the Holy Spirit.*" The word "moved" in this passage is a translation of the Greek word "*pero*," which means "to bear up or to carry." In other words, the prophets "spake" as they were being carried along by the wind of the Holy Spirit. As I ministered that evening, both my feet were firmly planted on the ground, but I could feel my spirit soaring; I was being born up and carried along on the wind of the anointing.

I began sharing the story of my life. Until that moment, I had never shared that portion of my testimony with anyone. Under the unction of the Holy Spirit, I began to share some things that were so painful to remember that I had not even spoken about them to my husband.

I began to weep as I moved across the platform talking about the pain of watching helplessly as my mother took beating after beating. I told of being nervous and frightened. I told of having panic attacks that left me gasping for air. Then I told of Christ's matchless love.

I told of His tender care, for a little girl; the only Believer in her house; a little girl who walked more than a mile to church even on cold snowy mornings rather than stay away from the house of God.

Up until that point, I thought I had been healed but that evening some deep hurts, some long festering wounds were exposed and the healing balm of God's love applied. At that moment, my healing was made complete and my ministry was birthed in me. You see, that is the way God works. He will often take the thing that has caused us the most pain and make it our ministry. The Apostle Paul said...

> *Blessed [be] the God and Father of our Lord Jesus Christ, the Father of sympathy (pity and mercies) and the God [Who is the Source] of every consolation and comfort and encouragement; Who consoles and comforts and encourages us in every trouble (calamity and affliction), so that we may also be able to console (comfort and encourage) those who are in any kind of trouble or distress, with the consolation (comfort and encouragement) with which we ourselves are consoled and comforted and encouraged by God*
>
> *2 Corinthians 1:3,4*

Paul said God has comforted us and made us able to comfort others with the same comfort. In other words, when

God heals us, He does so in a way that makes us able to minister the same kind of healing to others.

God has healed me from the pain and torment of childhood abuse, and birthed in me a ministry to others who have suffered similar things.

Hold On to Your Healing

In our church, we believe in praying for the sick according to James chapter five. Over the years, I have noticed something. There are those who come for prayer, receive healing and deliverance, then, in a short while, come back requesting prayer for the same affliction. What's going on with these people?

Well, its simple. These folks are not holding on to what they received from the Lord. Once the prayer of faith has been prayed, and their healing is manifest, they go back to doing the same thing that made them sick in the first place. They go back to the same poor diet. They go back to being a "couch potato." They go back to holding anger and resentment in their hearts. As a result, they re-open those old doors, allowing the enemy to come back in and torment them again. Each time he is cast out and allowed to come back, that person's condition gets worse.

When the unclean spirit is gone out of a man, he walketh through dry places, seeking rest; and finding none, he saith, I will return unto my house whence I came out. And when he cometh, he findeth it swept and garnished. Then goeth he, and taketh to him seven other spirits more wicked than himself; and they enter in, and dwell there: ant the last state of that man is worse than the first.

Luke 11:24-26 (KJV)

Once God has delivered you, do not go back to the things He has delivered you from. Do not go back to the same old eating and exercise habits. Do not go back to being angry and resentful. Do not spend time digging up the past with its old hurts and pain. Instead, get busy building a new and prosperous future in Christ.

You should stop hanging out with negative people. You know the ones I'm taking about. The ones who like to give life to those things that are "passed away" by gossiping about them, and glorying in them.

Seek out spiritual believers, those who speak the Word of God, and walk according to its precepts. These folks will help you stay free.

Get involved in the church, join the choir, become an usher or find some other work you can do in ministry. By all means attend worship as often as possible. Get involved in the teaching ministry of your church. Learn all you can. Prepare yourself for the day when God will use you to be a blessing to someone else. God may not call you to speak to large crowds, but we all have the opportunity to touch lives, one person at a time.

Place yourself under the tutelage of your spiritual leaders, your pastors. They will nurture you, train you and perfect you. Let me share with you the same exhortation that Jesus shared with Peter, "...*When you have been converted strengthen your brethren.*" You will experience more and more healing as you work to help others.

8

Life Is Not Over Yet

"Ok, so where do I go from here?" you ask. What direction and what purpose does my life have now? My past has been gloomy and full of trouble and despair. So, what does the future hold?

I can relate to these feelings. Your dreams and ambitions have been on hold; in fact, you may have felt utterly hopeless, until now. While on his bed of affliction, Job felt the same way.

> *My days are past, my purposes and plans are frustrated; even the thoughts (desires and possessions) of my heart are broken off.*
>
> *Job 17:11*

Job was not a victim of domestic violence, but many survivors can identify with Job. Abuse is a different kind of affliction, but an affliction, non-the-less. The despair and sorrow Job experienced in sickness, is not all that different from that felt by those living with daily abuse and pain.

Job had friends who did not understand his situation. They told Job that he must be to blame for the suffering he was experiencing. Job's wife was just as ignorant as his friends. She went so far as to tell Job to commit suicide by cursing God. In all this, Job held fast to his faith in God.

Because Job had the faith to patiently wait upon the Lord, his captivity was "turned." In the end, Job had more than he had in the beginning.

For the past nine years our ministry has sponsored a conference devoted to dealing with the issues of domestic violence and abuse. We have worked with several women's groups and shelters, allowing their clients to attend our meetings free of charge. We have seen both abusers and perpetrators delivered by the power of God. The one thing that has been disturbing in this is the fact that some of the organizations seem to have and anti-Christian bias.

We have seen women tremendously blessed and healed at our conferences. When they return to the shelter, they are discouraged from attending church. Some have even been shipped out to some other location so that our workers cannot follow up with them.

A person should not have to trade one kind of bondage for another. You do not have to go from isolation and control under an abusive spouse to isolation and control under people who are supposed to be helping you.

I'm well aware of the fact that the safety of the one escaping an abusive situation must be guarded. Steps must be taken to keep his or her whereabouts hidden from the perpetrator until authorities can deal with him or her effectively. Law enforcement officials warn that the most dangerous time for a survivor is when they try to get out. However, one should not be required to abandon their faith in order to get help.

This is where the church can be a blessing. I pray that churches will take up this cause and begin to provide places throughout the nation and around the world where women and men coming out of abusive situations can find the help they need in an environment where faith is recognized as the vital part of the healing process that it is. I pray that churches will...

- Expand education and awareness with regard to domestic violence, child abuse and sexual abuse
- Promote nonviolence and encourage individuals to report family violence
- Mandate training in domestic violence for ministers, teachers and counselors
- Establish and fund shelters for victims and their children
- Accompany victims to court. Walk with them through the sometimes intimidating legal process
- Develop a list of legal and counseling resources to which victims and perpetrators may be referred.

Job training and financial assistance are also often needed. Often when a person leaves a violent situation he or she is fortunate to make it out with nothing but the clothes on their back. Churches can provide resources to help survivors get back on track and get a fresh start in life.

Every possible precaution should be taken to ensure that victims of abuse get out and get out safely. God wants us to be safe from harm and danger but he also wants us to be spiritually and emotionally whole.

Listen, your life is not over yet! God is about to bless you in a big way, if you can believe Him. Look at what God said to the prophet Isaiah.

> *Arise from depression and prostration in which circumstances have kept you - rise to a new life! Shine (be radiant with the glory of the Lord) for your light has come, and the glory of the Lord has risen upon you!*
>
> *Isaiah 60:1*

I really believe the Spirit of the Lord is ministering to you even as you read these pages. I believe that you are being healed and delivered at this very moment. It is time, now to put the painful past behind you and arise to new life in Christ Jesus.

Arise from the gloom and darkness of the past and see the sunshine of new hopes and dreams. It is time to look beyond the pain and see a bright new day. Ephesians says, *"...be constantly renewed in the spirit of your mind, having a fresh mental and spiritual attitude."*

You no longer have to live with anger, bitterness, and resentment or with the situation that gave birth to them. You can become a new creation in Christ. You can put on a brand new nature and become a brand new person.

When God delivers us we are then ready to enter a season of gladness and rejoicing. If you know anything about birds, you know how happy they appear when the cold of winter is past. You can open the window, in the spring, and hear them chirping and whistling. I'm not gifted to interpret the tongues of birds but their singing is such a happy sound.

Now that your past is behind you, break forth into singing. I am always encouraged by the words of the apostle.

> *We are troubled on every side, yet not distressed; we are perplexed, but not in despair; Persecuted, but not forsaken; cast down, but not destroyed;*
> *1 Corinthians 4:8 (KJV)*

We may have been abused...but we are not shaken!

For more information about Abused But Not Shaken Ministry or to correspond with the author contact us at...

patricia.heathman@sbcglobal.net

You may also visit us online at...

http://www.patriciaheathman.org